All Kinds of Family

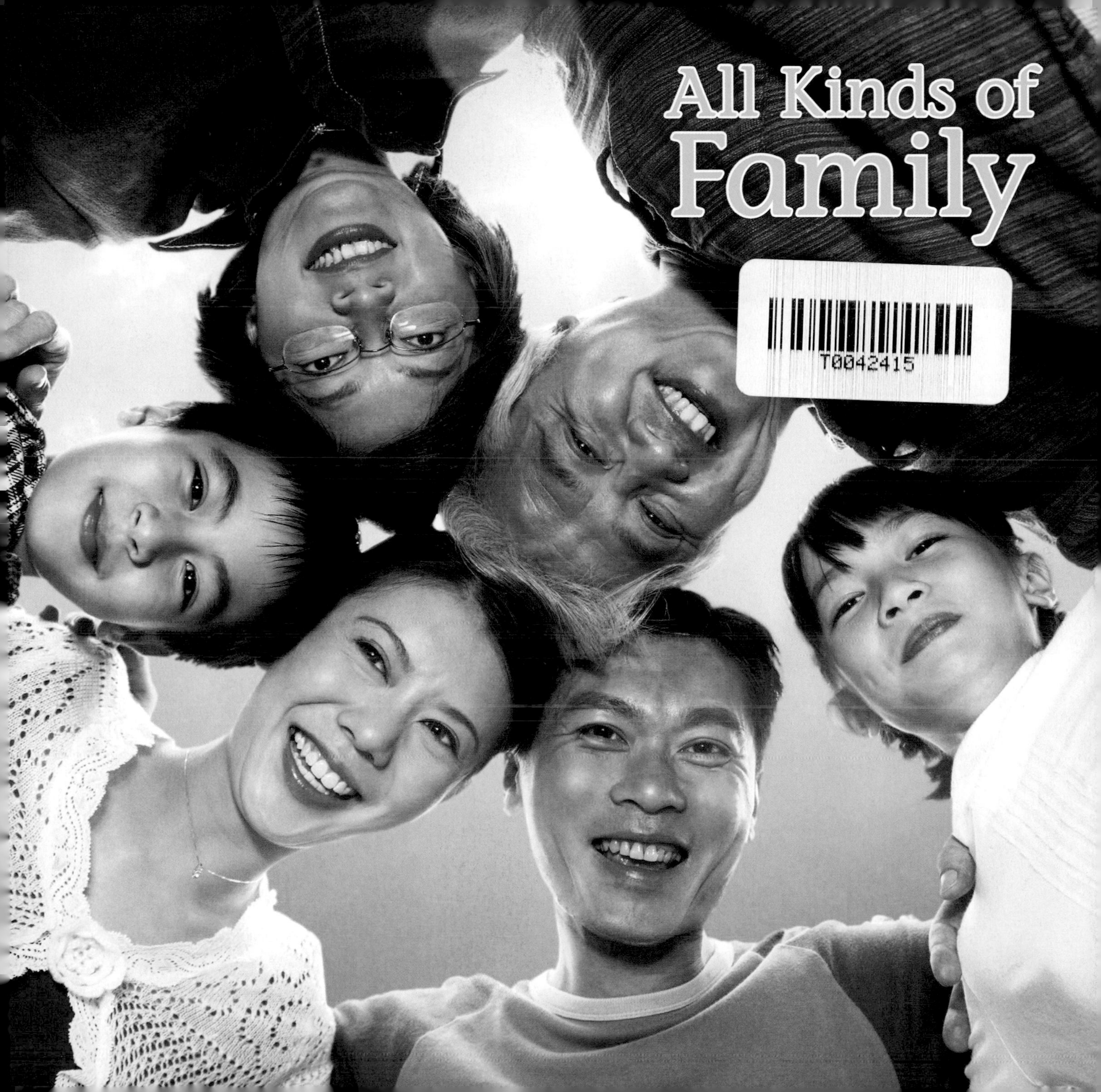

family

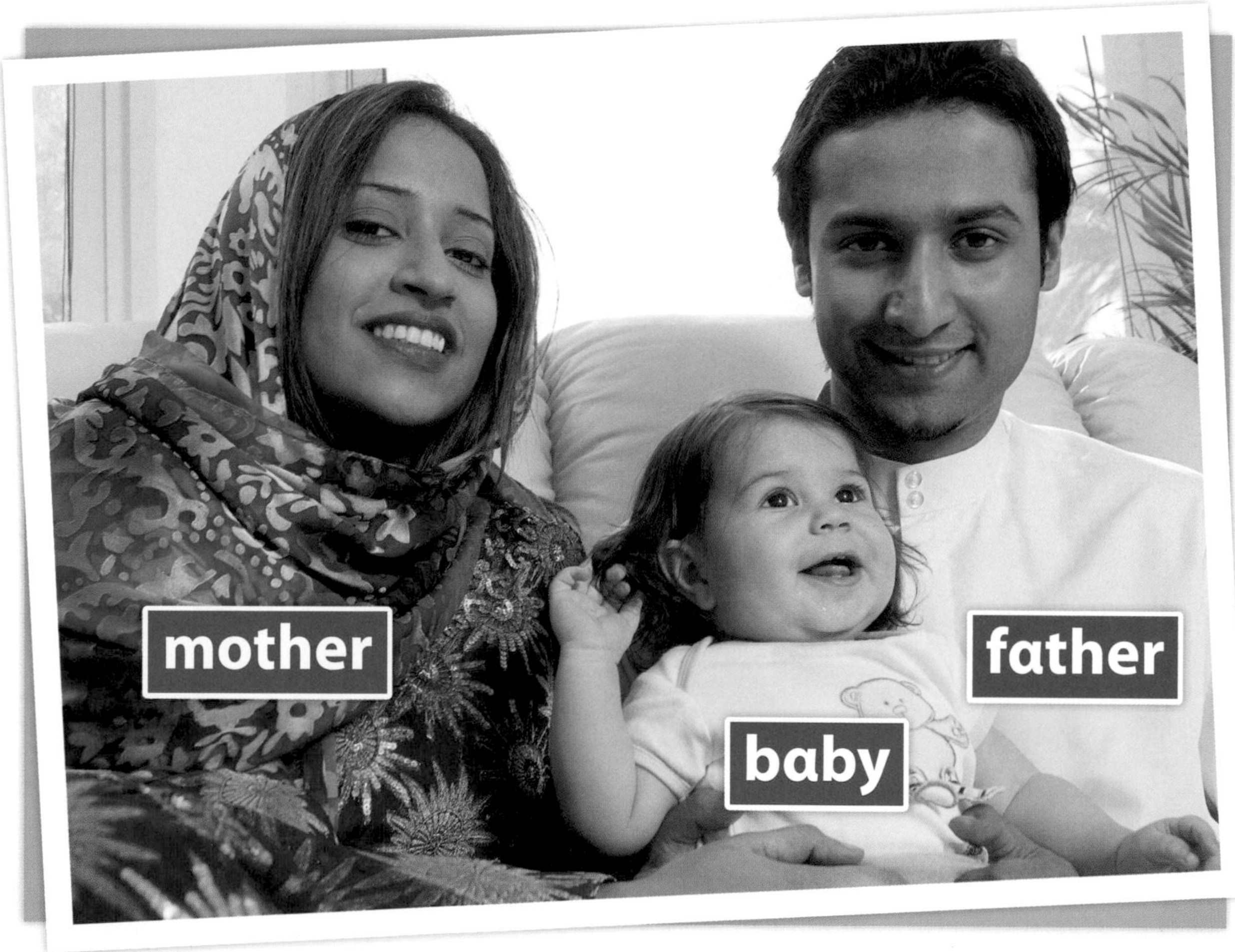
mother
father
baby

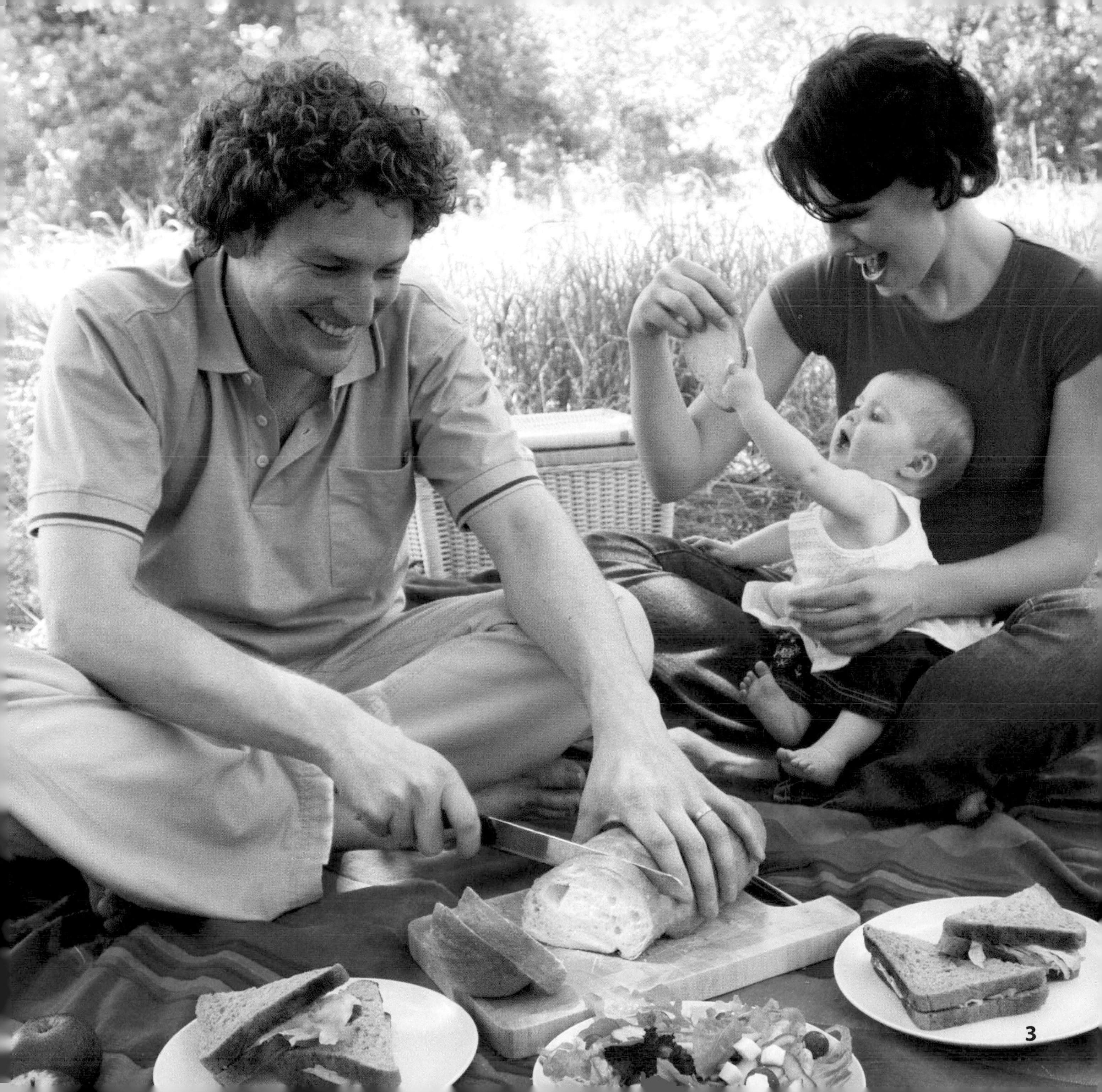

brothers

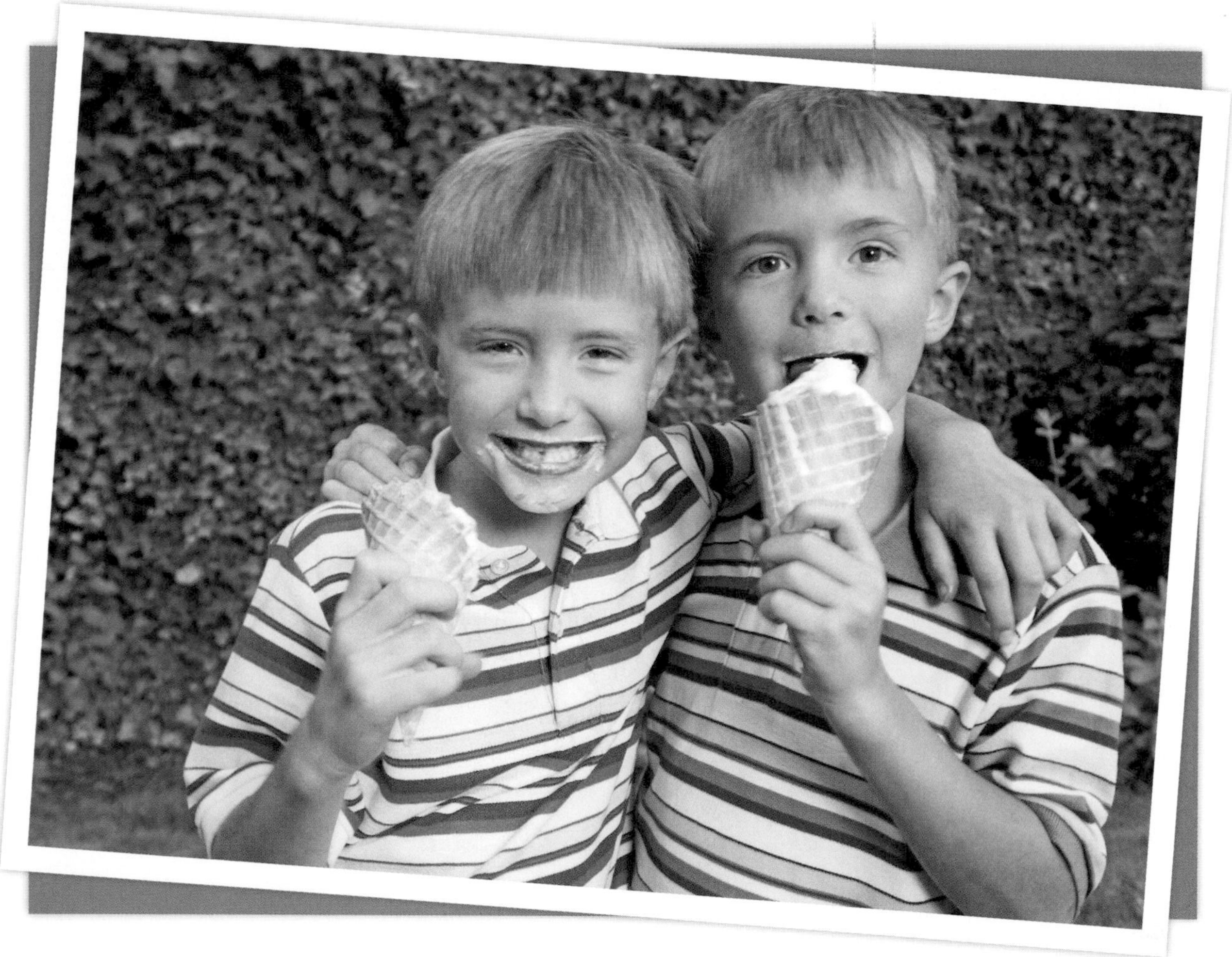

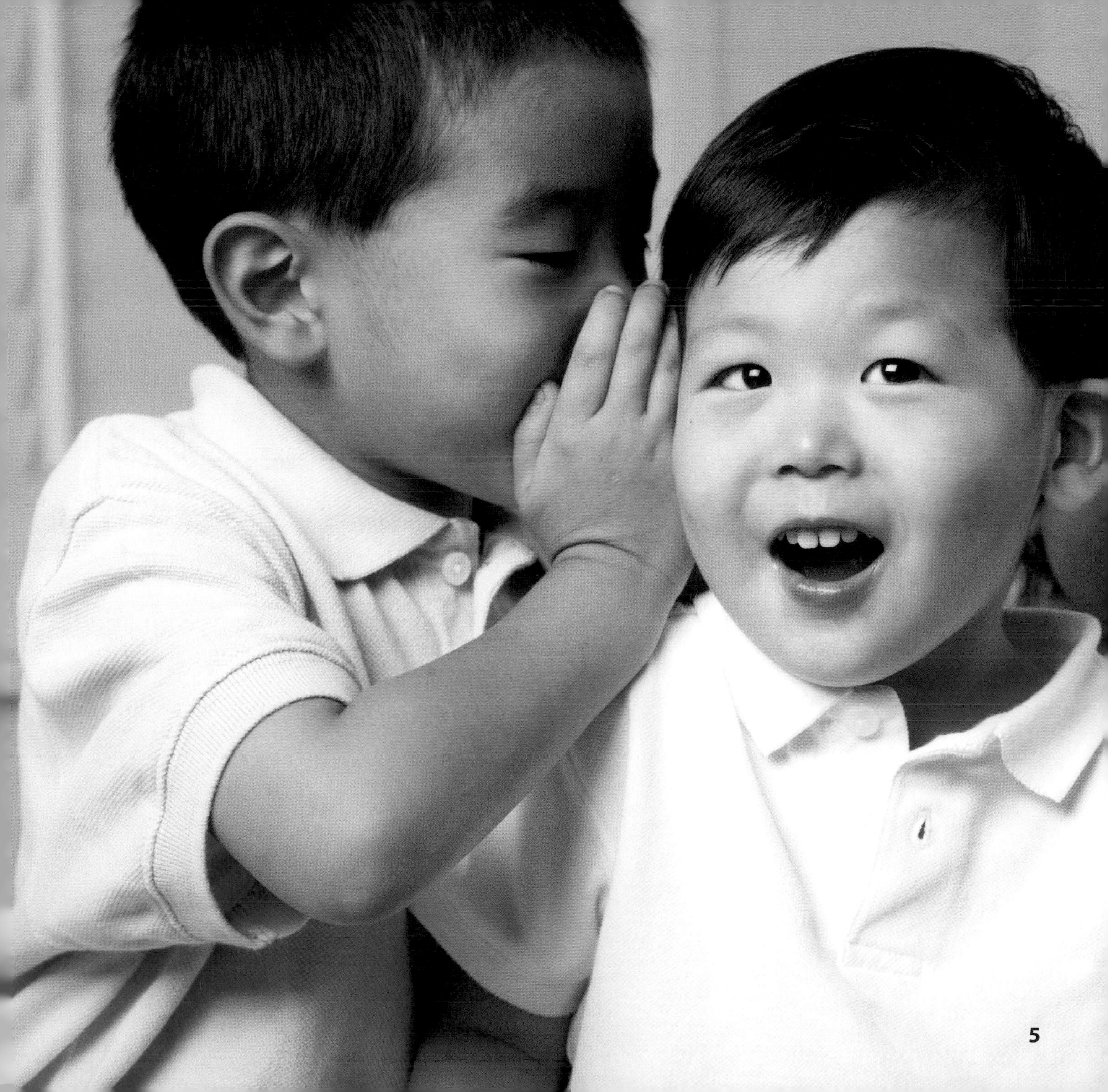

sisters

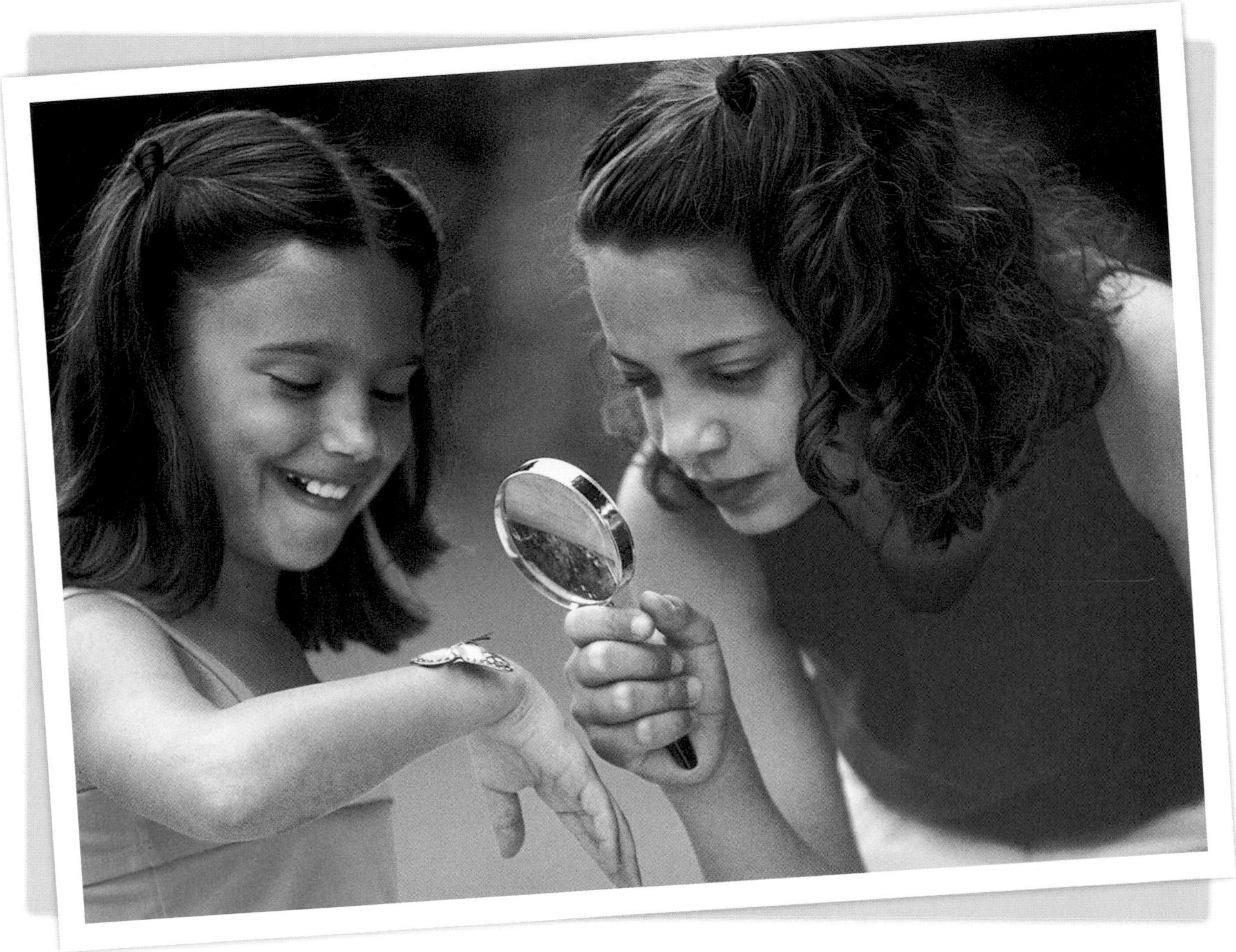

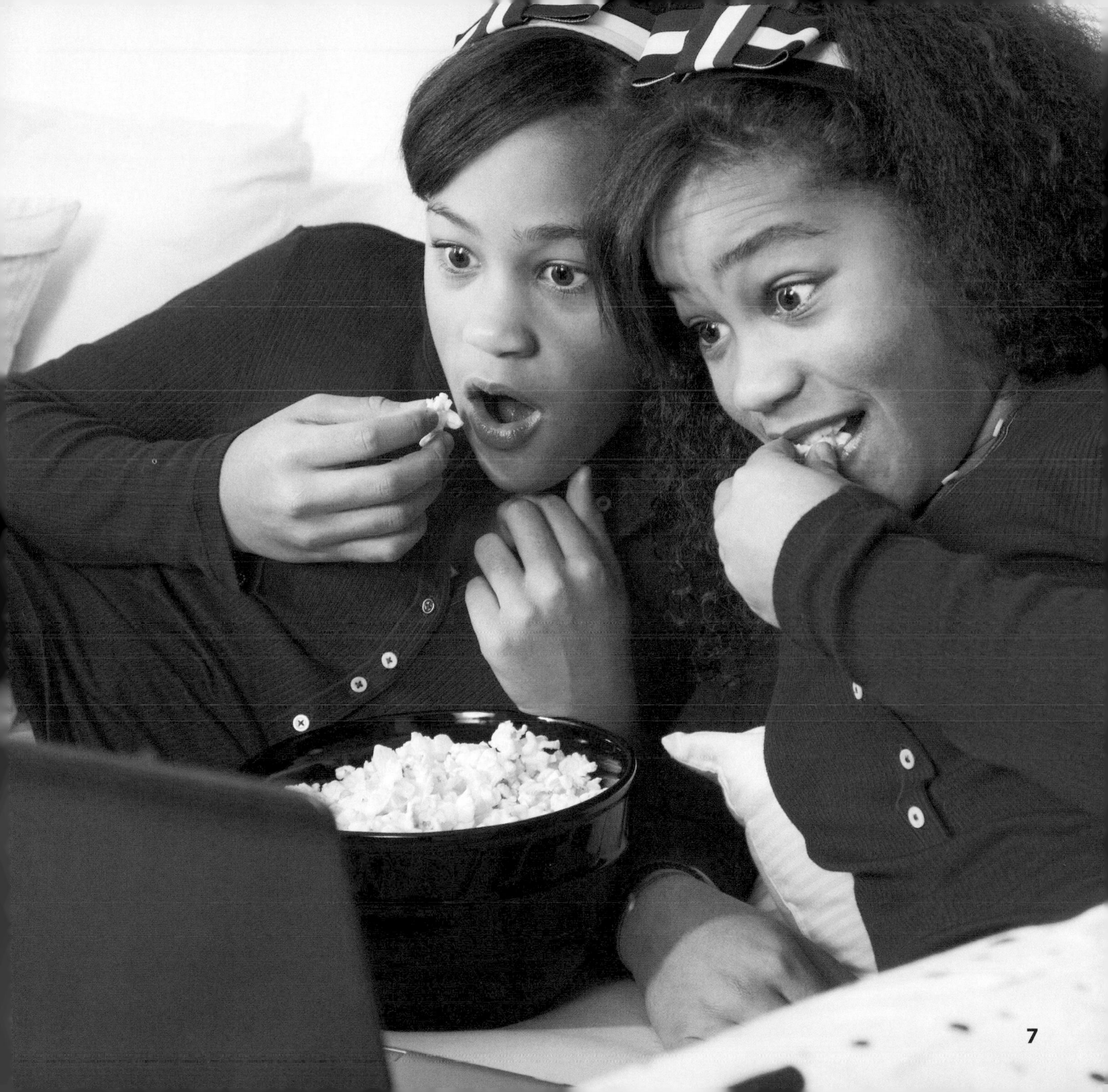

family

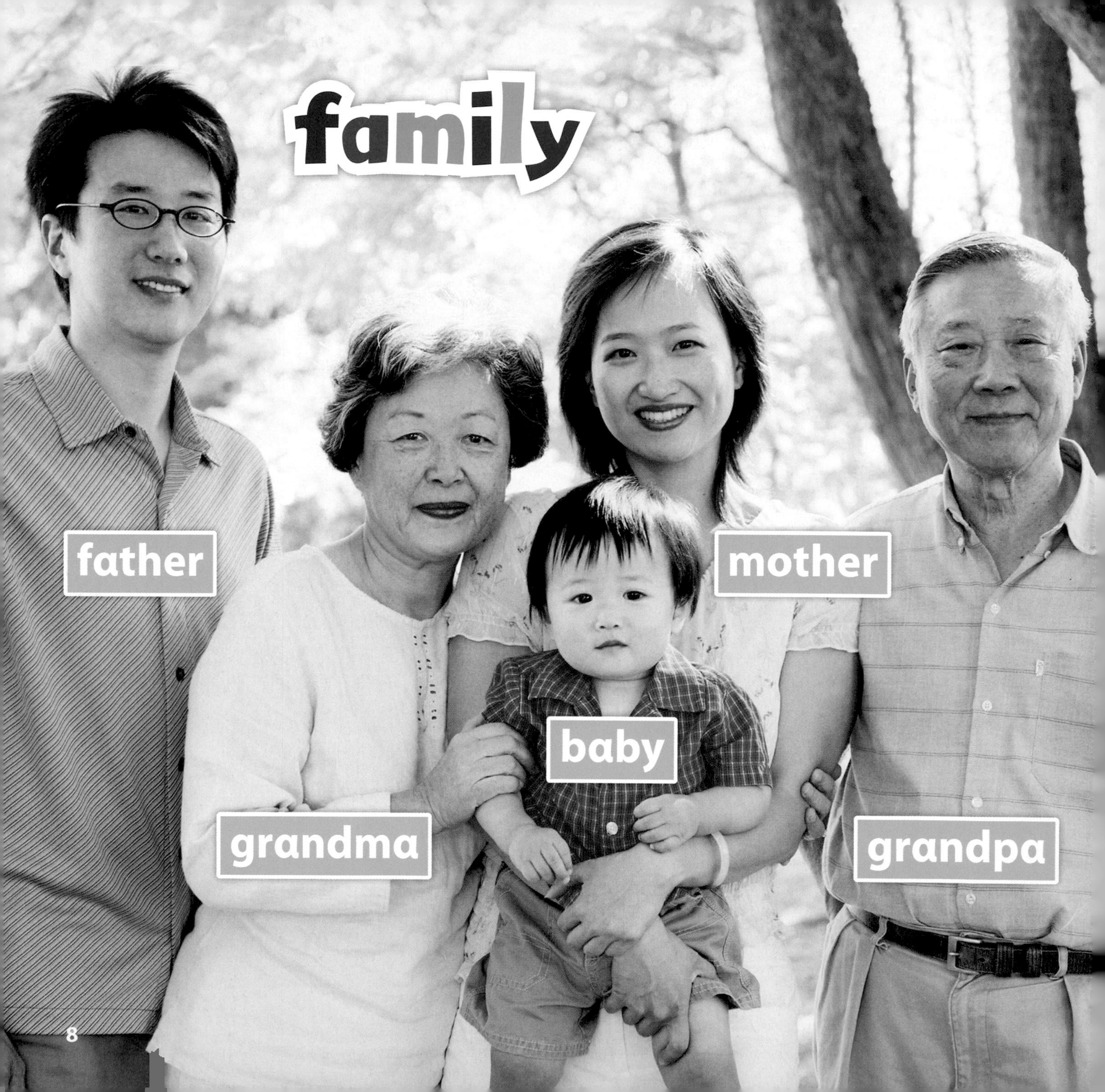
father
mother
baby
grandma
grandpa